Waterways

Ellen K. Mitten

Rourke
Educational Media
rourkeeducationalmedia.com

www.rourkeeducationalmedia.com

PHOTO CREDITS: © fanelliphotography: Title Page, 13; © Roberto A. Sanchez: 3, 23; © Dan Barnes: 5, 23; © Jordan Shaw: 7; © Edward Todd: 9; © David Parsons: 11, 23; © urban-photo: 15, 22; © Matthew Ragen: 17, 22; © westphalia: 19, 23;   © Paul Kline: 21, 22

Edited by Meg Greve

Cover design by Nicola Stratford bdpublishing.com
Interior design by Tara Raymo

Library of Congress Cataloging-in-Publication Data

Mitten, Ellen.
  Waterways / Ellen Mitten.
     p. cm. -- (Little world geography)
  ISBN 978-1-60694-420-2 (hard cover)
  ISBN 978-1-60694-536-0 (soft cover)
  ISBN 978-1-60694-587-2 (bilingual)
  1. Waterways--Juvenile literature. I. Title.
  HE381.M58 2010
  386--dc22
                                        2009005743

Printed in China, FOFO I - Production Company
  Shenzhen, Guangdong Province

rourkeeducationalmedia.com

customerservice@rourkeeducationalmedia.com • PO Box 643328 Vero Beach, Florida 32964

What are **waterways?**

Waterways are roads for **ships** to transport **goods** and people.

cargo ship

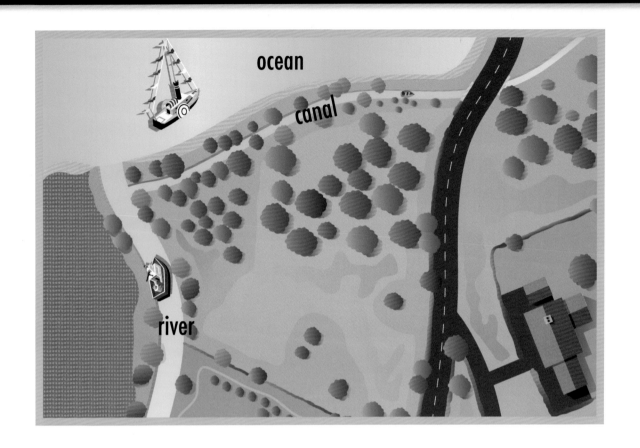

Rivers, **canals**, and **oceans** are waterways.

motorboat

river

Rivers were the first waterways to carry goods between cities.

barge

tugboat

Boats have carried goods and people to cities up and down some rivers for hundreds of years.

sailboat

Canals are waterways built by people. They connect two waterways together to transport goods quickly.

cabin cruiser

13

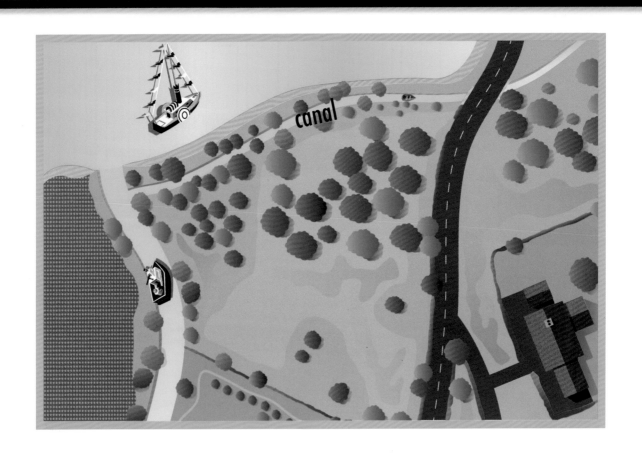

Small canals link rivers to cities.

rowboat

Bigger canals shorten the distance ships travel from one ocean to another ocean.

cargo ship

Huge canals shorten routes of oil **tankers** from one country to another country.

tanker

Rivers, canals, and oceans keep goods and people on the move all over the world. They are important waterways.

cruise ship

21

GLOSSARY

 **canals** (kuh-NALS): Channels that are dug across land. Canals connect bodies of water so that ships can travel between them.

 **goods** (GUDZ): Things that are sold, such as food, furniture, and clothing. Goods can also be things that are owned.

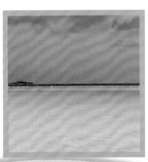 **oceans** (OH-shuhns): Oceans are the largest bodies of water on Earth. The water is salty. There are five major oceans: the Pacific, Atlantic, Indian, Arctic, and Southern.

 **rivers** (RIV-urs): Natural streams of fresh water that flow into lakes or oceans.

 **ships** (SHIPS): Large boats that can travel across deep water.

 **tankers** (TANG-kurs): Ships that are equipped with tanks for carrying liquids.

 **waterways** (WAW-tur-ways): Rivers, canals, or other bodies of water on which ships and boats travel.

Index

Websites to Visit

www.boatsafe.com/kids/navigation.htm

education.usace.army.mil/navigation/waterwy.html

kids.nationalgeographic.com

About the Author

Ellen K. Mitten has been teaching four and five-year-olds since 1995. She and her family love reading all sorts of books!